Shak Sto

Original stories by William Shakespeare

Retold by Chris Powling

Series Advisor Professor Kimberley Reynolds

Illustrated by Alan Marks

OXFORD
UNIVERSITY PRESS

Letter from the Author

When I was your age, I had a wonderful teacher called Miss Bowe. Miss Bowe loved stories. Whether she was telling them, reading them, or helping us write them, she was absolutely magical – especially if the story was by her favourite author, William

Shakespeare. So maybe it's not surprising that when I grew up I became a teacher myself, then a broadcaster and a writer. The spell cast by Miss Bowe has lasted all my life!

Here, then, is my retelling of three stories by Shakespeare. One of them, *Twelfth Night*, may make you laugh. One, *Julius Caesar*, may make you feel rather sad. One, *The Winter's Tale*, may make you wonder ... though you'll find some laughter, sadness and wonder in all three if you care to look. If they cast anything like the spell on you that Miss Bowe's stories cast on me, I'll be delighted.

Chris Powling

Twelfth Night

Sebastian and Viola were twins. They looked like each other. They sounded like each other. They even behaved like each other ... or so it seemed to everyone who knew them. 'It's lucky you're a boy and a girl,' people said. 'If you *dressed* like each other as well, we'd never tell you apart!'

The twins smiled at this.

Sometimes, you see – just for a joke – they did dress like each other. 'That's when we're double the trouble,' Viola grinned.

How right she was. It was dressing up like her brother which led to the biggest mix-up in their lives.

A stormy day it had been. A stormy day at sea, what's more. A gale-force wind and towering waves drove their ship closer and closer to the jagged shoreline.

Soon it was everyone for themselves as the doomed vessel splintered apart. When

Viola finally staggered to her feet on a lonely beach she let out a wail of dismay. 'Our ship's smashed to bits!' she cried. 'And where's my brother Sebastian?'

'He went overboard with the captain, Miss,' growled an old sailor stranded nearby. 'I saw them clinging to a broken spar. More than likely they landed further along the coast.'

'But what coast is it?'

'This is Illyria, lady. Ruled over by Duke Orsino. Look! Your trunk's been swept on the rocks. While I'm searching for other survivors, you should sort yourself out some dry clothes.'

'That's Sebastian's trunk not mine,' said Viola, sadly. 'But don't let me keep you from your duty.'

Already a plan was forming in her mind. A young woman who's all alone in a foreign country can have a very hard time of it. It's much easier for a young man. This gave Viola an idea. After all, it wasn't the first time she'd swaggered about in her brother's stuff. 'Why not try my luck now?' she asked herself. 'I'll put on Sebastian's hat and boots and breeches and tote that sword he's so fond of. I'll change my name, too. From now on I'll be *Cesario*. Who knows, maybe this Duke Orsino will give me a job in his household. Isn't that what Sebastian himself would do?'

To her relief, the plan worked.

Duke Orsino needed all the help he could get. He'd fallen in love with his neighbour, Countess Olivia, who refused to marry him till she'd got over the death of her father and her brother – at least seven years of mourning, she'd told him. No wonder he swooned around his palace all day. Every so often, he'd sigh heavily with a remark like, 'If music be the food of love, play on ... ' as if all he needed to keep himself going was some sort of song-sandwich.

Viola found it very boring. Or *Cesario* did, rather. For she was a young gentleman now, remember. In fact, she'd managed her disguise so cleverly that she was soon the Duke's favourite companion.

'A lad like you, Cesario, is just who I need to keep me from despair,' he groaned. 'I've opened the book of my secret soul to you.'

Cesario gritted her teeth. *How could such a bright, handsome man be so soppy?* she grumbled to herself. *Any moment now he'll be sending me off to tell this Countess Olivia how much he worships her and how much he longs for her to marry him!*

Oh dear.

It was as if she'd spoken the words out loud. A moment later, the Duke ordered her to do exactly that. 'My love, my happiness, my very life all depend on you, Cesario,' he wailed. 'Only a young man with your sharp wits can help me. Don't let me down, I beg you ... '

He looked so sad, and was so good-looking, Cesario's heart melted at once.

***

When Viola – sorry, *Cesario* – arrived at Countess Olivia's mansion she blinked in surprise. With its deer park and acres of garden, it was just as vast and luxurious as the Duke's own palace. But was this really a house in mourning for a dead father and a dead brother? Who was the roly-poly man, with a bushy beard, propped against a shady oak tree in the courtyard? And who was the skinny-ribbed fellow with floppy yellow hair sprawled out next to him? And why were they lazing about

so early in the day? 'Sir Toby Belch at your service, squire,' said the solid one, smoothing his beard.

'And I'm Sir Andrew Aguecheek,' the scrawny one piped up. 'Will you join us in a piece of cake? Maria here, the Countess's lady, will be happy to fetch it for you.'

'I don't think—' Cesario began.

She got no further.

The voice that had made her swing round was like a long streak of vinegar squeezed through a rusty pipe. 'What's going on here?' the newcomer sneered. 'Broad daylight and already party time?'

'And this is Malvolio,' Sir Toby sniffed. 'He's steward to my niece, the Countess, though you'd never guess it. He acts as if he's her master. He acts as if he's *my* master, come to that. Being such a goody-goody himself, he thinks all cakes should be banned.'

'Along with everything else that's *fun*,' said Maria, sharply.

From the look they gave each other, it was clear the Countess's lady and the Countess's steward were at daggers drawn. *But whose weapon was the sharper?* Cesario wondered. *And what was the letter Maria had hidden so quickly in her pocket when Malvolio first appeared? Had she been reading it aloud to Sir Toby and Sir Andrew?*

Cesario felt the pinch of bony fingers on her arm. 'Don't waste your time with riff-raff like this,' Malvolio hissed. 'Let me take you straight to the Countess, young man.'

The Countess wasn't quite what Cesario expected. True, she was as beautiful as the Duke was handsome. And true, she was moping on a window seat, dressed in funeral black, but her sad eyes still lit up at the sight of this good-looking young newcomer in his hat with its flowing plume, his boots and breeches of the finest leather and an elegant sword hanging at his side. 'Not more weeping and wailing from Duke Orsino,' she pretended to

yawn. 'Haven't I told him over and over again
it'll be years before I let myself marry ... and
when I do it certainly won't be to *him*.'

'That's all you have to say, my lady?'

'Not one word more, young sir.'

'His case is hopeless, then,' said Cesario,
briskly. 'I'll tell him nothing has changed since
last time.'

'No ... *wait*.'

'Wait, madam?'

'You will come back, won't you?'

'Come back?'

'To let me know he's not *too* upset,' said the Countess, hastily. 'I may not love him but I'd hate to crush him altogether.'

Cesario stared at her, baffled. Was this what everyone did here in Illyria – play some sort of teasing game? Why, from the dreamy look on the Countess's lovely face it was almost as if ...

No.

It wasn't possible.

Was it?

No, it wasn't – it definitely *wasn't*.

By the time she'd shut the gates of Olivia's deer park behind her, Cesario had almost managed to shake off the terrible thought which had wormed its way into her head. Suddenly, behind her, she heard the sound of stately footsteps which she recognized only too well.

'My mistress has required me to return this ring to you forthwith, sir' said Malvolio, loftily. 'She says it's yours and you left it behind in error.'

'Not me,' Cesario said at once.

'Of course it was you,' the steward snorted. 'Are you saying my mistress is mistaken? Are you refusing to take it back? Here, I've dropped the ring in the dust. Pick it up if you choose to do so ... or leave it for some passer-by or beggar to find.'

After Malvolio had stalked off, Cesario slumped to her knees in despair. The terrible thought was back in her head.

There was no denying it this time. 'It wasn't a mistake,' she choked. 'I was right the first time. Countess Olivia sent me the ring on purpose. Now look at the mess I'm in. I was so good at pretending to be a man, she's fallen in love with *me*!'

***

The sun was higher in the sky now. The oak tree in the Countess's courtyard cast shadows that were deeper and darker than ever. 'All the better to cover our plotting,' Sir Toby chuckled. 'And all the better to hide us while we watch that weasel Malvolio fall into our trap.'

'Will he have found the letter yet?' squeaked Sir Andrew.

'Oh yes,' said Maria. 'I left it out in the open on Malvolio's favourite walk. He'll spot the

handwriting at once – as close to my lady's as I could make it. He'll have read it a hundred times by now.'

'So he'll be convinced Countess Olivia is in love with him? And he'll be wearing the yellow tights she hates?'

'Probably wearing them already, Sir Toby.'

'And the cross-garters?'

'Already laced up, I expect.'

'And he really believes a lady like my niece could fancy the sort of man who dresses up in such frippery?'

Maria giggled. 'Sir Toby, he believes a lot more than that. For instance, he's convinced a stuck-up steward like him is fit to marry a Countess like her. Don't you remember what the letter told him?

"Some are born great
Some achieve greatness
Some have greatness thrust upon them."
I bet he's swallowed every word!'

'The villain!' exclaimed Sir Andrew. 'Why, even a knight of the realm like me can't be *completely* sure I deserve a wife like Olivia. Why else have I spent so much time here trying to catch her eye? And little good it's done me I'm sorry to say.'

'So far, my friend, only so far,' said Sir Toby, smoothly. 'No need to be downhearted. Your luck could change at any moment.'

'You think so?'

Sir Toby twirled his moustache. 'I *know* so,' he declared. 'Sure as cake is cake, fun is fun, and upstart prigs like Malvolio get ideas above their station. Trust me on that.'

'Trust me, you mean,' said Maria. 'And trust the letter I spent so much time in forging. Quick! Let's hide behind the oak tree. I can see His Royal Stewardship coming this way.'

***

At first the Duke said nothing when Cesario gave him the bad news. He was still droopy, yes. His handsome face was still woebegone. But somehow he didn't look quite as tragic as before. If anything, he seemed to her ... well, more *manly*. Cesario felt worse than ever. 'If only I could be womanly,' she muttered. 'I'd marry you myself and the sooner the better.'

There ... she'd finally said it.

For all his posing and moping, she couldn't deny any longer how fond of him she'd become.

Duke Orsino looked up. 'I'm sorry, Cesario,' he told her, dolefully. 'I'm afraid I missed what you were saying.'

'Nothing important I promise you, my lord. Just a stray thought that came into my head.'

'What thought was that?'

Cesario took a deep breath. 'About a girl who *was* in love,' she sighed. 'And didn't dare admit it to anyone.'

'What happened to her?'

'Nothing, my lord. Her life was a blank ever after.'

'Like mine,' Orsino shrugged. 'Except I've admitted my love to all the world. Cesario, young friend, go back to the Countess. Give her this brooch as one last token of how much I care for her.'

Cesario bowed and did as she was told. Now it was she who was woebegone. Between them, one way or another, the Countess's ring and the Duke's brooch would twist her future in Illyria into a neat, tight, impossible knot. Even the Duke sensed how she was feeling. As he watched her leave the palace to do his bidding, he was frowning in puzzlement.

***

Sir Toby, Sir Andrew and Maria were just in time. The tree in the courtyard, and its surrounding bushes, hid all three of them from sight yet gave them a perfect view of Malvolio.

And what a view it was.

Their main problem was not to burst out laughing. 'Have you ever seen such a poltroon?' Maria spluttered.

'Such a popinjay!' added Sir Andrew.

'Such a *smarty-pants*!' Sir Toby finished off.

By this, he meant the yellow tights and the cross-garters of course. Malvolio hopped skipped and jumped so prancingly across the courtyard in order to show these off, it was as if the flagstones were suddenly red hot under his feet. Maybe that's why he wafted the letter about in the air ... to cool down his own excitement. 'Oh, Mistress-mine!' he crooned. 'Oh, Angel of Illyria! Oh, Countess who can count true value – the value of someone as super-stewardly as I am! How wise you are to recognize my real worth! I was beginning to think it would never happen ...'

At this point, he twirled himself slowly on the spot so every side of him had a chance to catch the sunlight.

Behind the oak tree, the watchers could hardly bear it. Sir Toby was gagging himself with his beard, Maria was stuffing her mouth with her apron and Sir Andrew was chomping so wildly at his own stringy locks it was as if he badly needed a haircut and couldn't bear to wait for a barber. If only the Countess Olivia had been there. Then, their triumph would have been complete.

Suddenly, she *was* there.

From the main entrance of her mansion,
on the very top step, she stared in amazement
at her steward. Behind her was Cesario, still
holding the Duke's magnificent brooch.

Malvolio noticed it at once. A sickly,
wheedling grin spread across his face. 'Has he
brought that jewel for me, my precious one?' he
asked. 'An early gift for our wedding, perhaps?'

'Our wedding?'

'You and I bound together at last, Countess,' Malvolio smirked. '"Some are born great ... some achieve greatness ... some have greatness thrust upon them." I shall treasure those words forever, sweet madam. Written in your own hand as part of this very letter.'

'Not written by me,' said Olivia, icily. 'Are you mad, Malvolio? Has the sun gone to your head? Maria, fetch help. Convey this man to a safe, dark room with a lock on the door. He can stay there till he's recovered his wits. No, not another word, Malvolio! In the meantime ... in the meantime ... '

She bit her lip as she turned to Cesario. 'Dear, dear Cesario,' she begged, taking his hand. 'Will you forgive this upset in my household? Please don't make this your last visit.'

Cesario bowed. 'My master the Duke—'

'Oh fiddlesticks! Who cares about your master the Duke?'

'I do,' said Cesario, sadly.

This was too much for Countess Olivia. In tears, and with a swish of her black funeral skirt, she disappeared into the house.

'Did you see that?' bleated Sir Andrew. 'She's fonder of the Duke's manservant than she is of me! Now this Cesario has gone she'll stay indoors longing for his next visit.'

'So now's your chance!'

'What chance?'

'To snuff out this whippersnapper Cesario once and for all and clear your way to marriage with my niece.'

'How will I do that?'

Sir Toby smiled with satisfaction at his own cleverness. 'You challenge him to a duel,' he announced.

Sir Andrew went pale. He flopped limply against the oak tree like a puppet whose strings have been cut. 'A duel?' he gulped. 'You mean a proper duel? With swords and such? One of us might get hurt!'

'Both of you might get hurt,' nodded Sir Toby.

'*Both* of us?'

'Anything can happen in a duel. What's important is to make sure it's Cesario, rather than you, who gets hurt the most.'

'Hurt the most ... ' said Sir Andrew, faintly.

***

They caught up with Cesario on the road outside the Countess's gate. 'Stand fast, young feller-me-lad!' boomed Sir Toby. 'My noble comrade here has a score to settle with you.'

'With me?' said Cesario, baffled. 'I hardly know him.'

'You'll soon know him better, sir ... not to mention the cut and thrust of his knightly sword as it swirls around your ears. He'll crop them so close to your head your hat will fall over your eyes!'

'Have I done him some harm without

knowing it?'

'Not for much longer,' said Sir Toby, darkly. 'Aguecheek, kindly show this brat, this whelp, this puppy dog the colour of your blood ... of your blade, I mean. Draw your weapon, sir!'

'I will,' yelped Sir Andrew. 'I will.'

But he couldn't draw it. Not with hands so shaky he could barely get a grip on the sheath let alone the sword itself. At last, after a dozen tries, it slid out so unexpectedly it smacked its owner across the face. 'Ah! Ah!' Sir Andrew shrieked. 'I'm wounded! I'm mortally wounded!'

'A scratch, sir. A mere scratch, I promise you,' said Sir Toby. 'Not worth a dab of Maria's apron. Besides, take a look at your opponent. He's just as scared as you are!'

This was true.

Not having wielded a sword before – not ever – Cesario was having trouble with her own weapon. Two-handed, she wagged it this way and that in front of her. She hardly knew which was more likely – stabbing Sir Andrew or stabbing herself. Every time their blades clashed, they let out a whoop of alarm as if the sound itself was a deadly blow. It was anybody's guess which of them would be the victor. That's if there was a victor. This circling, shuffling dance of near hit and near miss could have gone on for the rest of the day till they both collapsed, exhausted.

It was a third sword which stopped them – cutting across their own. A rough, outdoor voice, used to the wind and the waves, rang out. 'Gentlemen, lower your weapons! This is too fine a day for fighting.'

A sailor, was he?

A captain, rather, to judge by his air of command. He stepped back as their swords clattered on the roadway. With his own sword, he saluted Sir Andrew. Then, with a glare, he saluted Cesario. 'I've been looking for you everywhere,' he said, flushed with anger. 'Why weren't you at our meeting point to repay the money I lent you?'

'Meeting point?' said Cesario. 'What meeting point? And what money are you talking about, sir?'

The captain's face hardened. 'Shame on you, Sebastian,' he growled. 'To cheat me now after I saved your life.'

'After you saved my life, sir?'

Cesario broke off.

As the captain sheathed his sword in disgust, Cesario suddenly understood. 'He thinks I'm Sebastian,' she whispered. 'He must be the captain the old sailor saw rescuing my brother. Sebastian must be alive!'

'Cesario!' came a shout.

'Duke Orsino?'

The Duke pulled up his horse in a cloud of dust. 'Forgive my impatience, good Cesario,' he said. 'I couldn't wait any longer for your return. How did the Countess Olivia respond to—'

Now it was his turn to break off.

He lifted a trembling finger towards the Countess's front gate. 'Why, there's my lady,' he said, bewildered. 'And there ... there's another you, Cesario! Heaven help me! I'm seeing you twice over!'

They were all seeing Cesario twice over. For coming towards them, hand in hand with Olivia, was a young man who wore a hat with a flowing plume, boots and breeches of the finest leather and a sword by his side just like

Cesario's. Cesario gave a gasp of joy. 'It's my
twin brother,' she exclaimed. 'It's Sebastian!'

Nobody spoke because nobody could believe
their eyes.

Here were two young men so alike in every
detail it was impossible to tell them apart.
'Hello!' Sebastian grinned. 'Trust my twin sister
Viola to turn up safe and sound, and dressed
just like me!'

'Your twin sister Viola?' said the Duke.

'Your twin sister Viola?' echoed the Countess. 'No wonder I mistook you for her when I saw you from my window.'

'And made me late for my meeting with the captain!' Sebastian added. 'Not that I tried very hard to get away. Countess, you're like a wonderful stranger I've known all my life ... '

'And you, Viola?' Duke Orsino murmured. 'Are you like a wonderful stranger I've known all my life ... but in disguise?'

Viola blushed. 'I wore my brother's clothes for safety, my lord. Not because I wanted to.'

'Clever,' said the Duke. 'And brave ... '

Was he in love with her already? Or did that come later when she was dressed as a woman again?

For soon the grandest of double weddings was announced: Sebastian to Countess Olivia and Viola to Duke Orsino. All of Illyria was invited and accepted the invitation gladly ... except, that is, for a certain bony steward with a vinegary voice.

He tore his invitation to bits and stomped off muttering, 'I'll be revenged on the whole pack of you!' Still, who cared if Malvolio stayed away? It meant more cakes and fun for the rest of them.

And there the story ends.

Mind you, it's never been forgotten. Who could forget the story of a shipwreck, a pair of marooned twins, a Duke, a Countess, a duel and a glorious trick played on a stuck-up steward ... especially with the happiest of happy endings. Why, it's a story fit for Christmas!

Now there's a thought.

A story as magical as this, so full of fun and laughter, could top off Christmas perfectly. Some people even say, and they're probably right, that's why Shakespeare called it *Twelfth Night*.

Julius Caesar

Julius Caesar was back in Rome.
Every Roman in the city knew this.
How could they have missed the news of his
latest battle, his latest triumph? Why else
would every statue be hung with garlands, every
window draped with flowers? Even the spring
breeze around the Forum seemed to whisper
'Caesar-Cacsar-Caesar'.

Or was it 'Success-Success-Success'?

No wonder he was smiling as he waved to the crowds who cheered him down every street. 'Thank the Gods not me,' he told them. 'The victory was theirs not mine – theirs and Lady Luck's!'

'It was yours, Caesar, *yours*!'

'My men then – my brave, lion-hearted men. True Romans every one of them. Look at their dented armour! Look at their blood-stained weapons! Look at the prisoners they took and the gold they captured to fill the city's coffers. Without them I'm nothing!'

'You're everything, Caesar, *everything*!'

'I'm a man, that's all,' Caesar insisted. 'A man no better or worse than other men.'

'The best, Caesar!' roared the crowd. 'The very best!'

Caesar sighed and shook his head but the smile never left his lips. Not even when his eye fell on the old soothsayer in the ragged cloak who peered out at him from an alleyway. 'Have you something to say to me, old man?' he asked. 'Some fortune you want to tell?'

'*Your* fortune, Caesar,' came the reply.

Caesar's smile tightened. 'Speak now, then – quickly. As you see, I'm leading this procession to the Capitol.'

The soothsayer pulled his cloak around him. He licked his lips and gave a hard dry cough as if his own words stuck in his throat. 'Caesar,' he growled. 'Beware the ides of March.'

'The ides of March?'

Caesar's smile was flinty now. The ides of March began the next day, on March the fifteenth, when the full moon always brought trouble, people said. This was nonsense, of course. Just superstition, that's all. How dare this scruffy fellow spoil the homecoming of a man who was ... who was ... 'no better or worse than other men,' Caesar told himself as if he believed it.

***

Some Romans weren't so sure. Cassius, for instance – a thin, hawk-faced senator with a wary glint in his eye. 'See?' he said. 'He's fishing the crowd for compliments – teasing them by pretending he's ordinary. Ordinary? Caesar? For him, ordinary is an insult. For him even *extraordinary* isn't enough! There's only one thing Caesar longs for. He wants to become top dog with the whole world as his kennel.'

'You think so?' murmured Brutus.

'I *know* so! And I'm not the only one. Ask Casca. Ask Cinna. Ask Decius, Trebonius, Ligarius and Metellus. Ask anyone who loves Rome as a republic, as a democracy of men who are free and equal!'

Brutus eyed his old friend, thoughtfully. 'And Caesar doesn't love Rome as we do? You can prove that?'

'Oh yes ... '

Cassius looked quickly over his shoulder. This side-doorway just off Rome's main square looked safe enough to him. No risk of being overheard here. 'Aren't you forgetting the offer of the crown?' he whispered.

'Ah,' said Brutus.

For weeks he'd been worried about this. And – yes – he had been trying to forget it. 'Remind me,' he said, grimly.

Cassius sniffed in disgust. 'Three times they asked him. "Become our king, Caesar!" they begged. "We want you as our king to rule

us as long as you live! Don't refuse us, Great Caesar!"'

'But he did refuse them, Cassius.'

'Twice, yes. Twice he waved them away – all shyness and embarrassment. But not the third time. The third time he hesitated.'

'The third time he fainted,' Brutus said. 'From his old complaint, the falling sickness. He collapsed, foaming at the mouth.'

'So you do remember,' said Cassius, smoothly. 'His young friend Mark Antony cradled him in his arms while the mob shouted, "King! King! King! We want Caesar for our king!"'

'And still he refused them, Cassius.'

Cassius lifted an eyebrow. 'Till next time, yes. Till next time when perhaps he won't collapse ... '

Brutus looked away. His kindly, intelligent face was troubled. Caesar was his friend, too. He knew him well and admired him greatly – as a soldier, as a leader, as a Roman. But what kind of a Roman? As the champion of a city whose citizens were free and equal? Or as the champion of his own vanity? With Caesar it could be either. More and more senators agreed with Cassius that he must be stopped whatever the cost.

Whatever the cost ...

Brutus gritted his teeth. 'This meeting of yours,' he said. 'With Casca, Cinna, Decius, Trebonius, Ligarius and Metellus, you say. When have you called them together, Cassius?'

'Tonight, Brutus. There's no time to be lost.'

'Bring them to my house, then,' Brutus said. 'At midnight.'

Cassius nodded at once. His face was as blank as a page predicting the future. Even his eyes had lost their knowing gleam. Nobody could have guessed – especially the open and generous Brutus – that this was exactly what Cassius had wanted all along.

***

That night, the storm which had been brewing all day finally broke. Thunder clattered over a brooding, starless sky; lightning flashed jaggedly across a city now bright, now dark; rain fell incessantly as if it meant to fall forever – on the Capitol, on the Forum, on the Senate House, on every square and street and alley. It was a night to be indoors, under cover, out of sight.

This suited the plotters perfectly – Casca, Cinna, Decius, Trebonius, Metellus, Ligarius, Cassius – and now, to everyone's relief, Brutus. Brutus the good, Brutus the true, Brutus the man of integrity whom every Roman loved, had joined their cause.

It suited Brutus, too, when they'd finally slipped away into the shadows. Now he must face his loving wife Portia. How could he tell her what had been decided? He hardly dared tell himself.

It even suited Caesar, in his villa, on this misery of a night. It seemed to confirm the recent omens – every one of them bad – which, taken together, were enough to unsettle any man however strong in battle. 'The warning from the old soothsayer ... ' he murmured.

'And the sacrifice you made to the Gods,' added his wife, Calphurnia. 'Of an animal whose heart turned out to be missing! That's the worst possible sign, Caesar. As for my dream ... '

She shuddered.

Caesar had to agree. 'My statue spouting blood,' he nodded. 'With Roman citizens washing their hands in it. Calphurnia, I hear what you're saying. I'll spend tomorrow here at home.'

'You promise?'

'When Decius comes to fetch me I'll tell him the Senate can do without me for a day or two. After all—'

He got no further.

Decius had arrived early and listened to Caesar with his usual charm. 'The choice is yours, mighty Caesar,' he bowed. 'You must do as you think fit. Though I'm surprised you don't see the dream differently. Surely the Romans in Calphurnia's dream are drawing on your blood for health and happiness! That's how I interpret it. Why, I've heard the senators have something special to offer you today: a crown, I do believe … '

Caesar stiffened.

Instantly, he was his public self again. Even his voice had changed. 'You're right, Decius,' he declared. 'A curse on this dreadful tempest! Who'd have thought it could unnerve a man like me? Have I ever been afraid of man or beast or *weather*? Cowards die many times before their deaths. The valiant never taste of death but once.'

'And who is more valiant than Caesar?' Decius smiled.

He smiled all the way to the Senate House

where the other conspirators were waiting. As the two of them passed the rain-washed alleyway which was home to the old soothsayer, Caesar smiled, too. 'The ides of March are come,' he said, cheerfully.

'Ay, Caesar, but not gone,' the old man replied.

***

Brutus took a long, hard look round the Senate House.

He saw senators like himself in their white and purple robes. He saw the red-cloaked tribunes of the people. He saw soldiers standing tall in their metal-studded leather alongside eager, wide-eyed citizens jostling with each other to catch the attention of someone important.

Brutus felt a surge of pride.

For this was the Senate doing its job. And what a job it was: Romans taking their turn

to rule other Romans under the Roman law –
the strongest and fairest parliament of equals
the world had ever seen. Cassius was right,
wasn't he? A king would ruin this. Even a king
as strong, as gifted and as driven as their old
friend Caesar would ruin this.

These were the thoughts in Brutus's head.
His heart was another matter.

Suddenly, he sensed someone by his side.
Cassius, as sharp as ever, was tugging at his
robe. 'Everything and everyone is in place,' he
hissed. 'Are you ready, Brutus?'

'As ready as I'll ever be,' Brutus said.

When it came, the killing was over in a
flash. To be precise, the flash of thirty-three
stab wounds from eight separate assassins.
Caesar reeled back, too surprised to defend
himself. It was the last blow which hurt him
most. He gaped like a fish jerked from a river
with a hook in its throat. Already his eyes were
glazed by death. 'You too, Brutus?' he gasped.

They were his last words. After that he

lay still. Every inch of his senator's robe was spattered with blood.

By now, with people fleeing in panic, a space had opened round the conspirators. 'We must escape!' one of them blurted. 'Our weapons are evidence. We'd better hide them.'

'We do no such thing!' Brutus snarled. 'We did this for Rome, didn't we, not for our own gain. We stay here and explain ourselves to anyone who'll listen. That way—'

He broke off as something caught his eye.

There, slumped against a pillar for support, was the young Mark Antony. His handsome face was stricken. He looked half as dead as Caesar and half as alive as the statue which towered over him. Cassius lowered his voice. 'He's trouble!' he hissed. 'We must kill him.'

'And make this a massacre?' Brutus said. He waved the thought away. 'You're safe with us, young man,' he promised. 'We are men you can trust. If it's your wish, approach your master and say your farewell.'

'Thank you, sir.'

Mark Antony bent over the body. Nobody heard the words he whispered in Caesar's ear but when he stood up he bowed low to Brutus. 'Thank you again,' he said. 'Will you grant me one thing more?'

'If I can.'

'To speak at Caesar's funeral, sir. I owe him that for all the favours ... all the kindness ... he always showed me.'

'See?' spat Cassius. 'It's a trick, I tell you.'

'Not if I speak first, Cassius.'

Cassius hesitated.

In that case, what harm could come of it? Mark Antony had barely made a speech in his life. Brutus, though – famed for his honesty and modesty – was one of the most popular speakers in the Senate.

Reluctantly, Cassius nodded. 'Go ahead, then,' he said out loud.

The bow Mark Antony gave him was even lower than his bow to Brutus. Julius Caesar would have smiled if he'd seen it.

***

The city was in a state of shock. Their hero was dead. No more victories from Caesar; no more parades; no more Roman holidays. Instead, his body lay in state outside the Capitol covered in a cloth of gold. 'How did this happen?' people wailed. 'Who did this?'

'Brutus was their leader, they say.'

'Brutus? Gentle Brutus? He was one of Caesar's closest friends!'

'So he must have had good reason.'

'Good reason? For murdering great Caesar? What kind of reason would that be, may I ask?'

It was a question everyone was asking. The crowd around the Capitol was in an ugly mood as it gathered for an answer. That's if any answer could be heard above the vicious muttering which filled the air ... like the low growl of an attack dog about to slip its leash.

Then Brutus stepped forward.

At once, there was silence. Was it the sadness of his face that hushed them? Or the blood-encrusted sword he made no attempt to hide? Then again, it may have been his voice – his clear, ringing voice – the voice of a man who always told the truth, however painful. 'Good people,' he said. 'Hear me out before you judge. No one in this city loved Caesar more than I did. So why did I strike him down? Because I loved Rome more ... '

His words were plain and simple. Caesar himself would have nodded in agreement as Brutus described his friend's outstanding strengths ... and his one fatal flaw. 'His ambition,' Brutus finished off, tight-lipped.

'It would have destroyed us all in the end.'

The silence, as he stepped back from the rostrum, had changed. Somehow it was louder now and more welcome than any burst of applause. Cassius and the other plotters began to relax.

Now it was Mark Antony's turn.

Taking his time, he waited till he was sure every eye was on him. Was this the young man who'd barely made a speech in his life? 'Friends,' he said, almost apologetically. 'Romans, countrymen ... I come to bury Caesar, not to praise him. Brutus says Caesar was ambitious. And Brutus is an Honourable Man – so are they all, all Honourable Men – which must mean they were right to kill him. Let me remind you of Caesar's *ambition* ... '

That's when his list began. He used the word 'ambition' over and over again linked with a mention of Brutus as an Honourable Man. His voice had an edge to it now which his listeners didn't miss.

Nor did they miss the climax of his speech. 'If you have tears,' he told them. 'Prepare to shed them now.'

And he read Caesar's will.

Was it genuine?

By the time Mark Antony finished, nobody cared if it was genuine or not. 'Seventy-five drachmas for every citizen in Rome,' he announced.

'Also, for their enjoyment, his private gardens on this side of the River Tiber – its walks, its shady spots, its newly-planted orchards – to be kept by you and your children forever. Now there's *ambition* for you.'

He'd done his work well. The crowd was stunned. But not for long. Already their anger at the conspirators, at the so-called Honourable Men, was rising, was spreading, was brimming over.

The attack dog had slipped its leash.

***

Rome was now out of control. Some citizens hid themselves in terror. Others roamed the streets smashing statues and monuments which were still hung with flowers and garlands for their hero's homecoming. But the worst of them simply wanted revenge. 'Who are you?' they demanded of a man hovering on his own doorstep.

'Me?' the man yelped. 'I'm Cinna.'

'Cinna? You're Cinna? He's one of the plotters who butchered Caesar, isn't he? Kill him!'

'No, no!' the man stammered. 'That's Cinna the senator – not me! I'm Cinna the poet!'

'Then sing your own death song, poet.'

Cinna the senator had more luck. Along with Cassius, Casca, Trebonius, Ligarius, Decius, Metellus and the reluctant Brutus, somehow he managed to escape in the city's confusion. A hundred other senators, who had nothing to do with the murder in the Senate House, paid for it with their lives.

Brutus and Cassius had no choice now. Mark Antony had made his move. With Caesar's adopted son Octavius, and an experienced soldier called Lepidus, he'd formed a partnership: to gather an army as their back-up and rule the city of Rome themselves.

'Not one king but three,' snapped Cassius. 'We must raise our own army or Rome as a republic will disappear forever.'

'I suppose we must,' said Brutus, wearily.

It was the outcome he'd dreaded. He was dizzy with grief. He'd just heard that Portia, his beloved wife, had killed herself by swallowing hot coals. The strain of recent events had been too much for her. They were almost too much for Brutus. But how could he and Cassius give up now, with Rome under a worse threat than ever? They must *organize* and fight on.

Their task wasn't easy.

For hours they wrangled over equipment, over tactics, over the order of battle and even over which of them – Brutus or Cassius – should be the general in charge.

At times they almost came to blows. 'Remember, this isn't the might of Rome pitted against an enemy,' Cassius pointed out. 'This is the might of Rome pitted against itself.'

'Civil war,' said Brutus, bleakly.

So it was that under a blood-red sunset on the plain of Philippi, the army of Brutus and

Cassius, and the army of Mark Antony and Octavius Caesar, were camped against each other. Now was the time to rest before the battle began at sunrise. Yet it was long after midnight when Brutus and Cassius fell into each other's arms, worn out by last-minute planning. 'Luck be with you tomorrow, old friend,' said Cassius, in tears.

'And with you, Cassius,' Brutus said. 'Most of all, let luck be with Rome.'

'With Rome,' Cassius agreed.

Alone at last, Brutus tossed and turned on his couch. The flap of canvas, the creak of a tent pole, the snicker of a horse tethered outside ... the slightest sound was enough to keep him from sleep. His brain was as wide awake as it had ever been. So how could he be dreaming when the blood-stained figure of Julius Caesar slid out of the shadows? Brutus sank back in horror. 'Is it really you?' he gasped. 'Are you still alive?'

'Alive enough,' Caesar whispered. 'But not in this life. You'll see me tomorrow, Brutus. Here at Philippi.'

'At Philippi,' Brutus said.

A candle flickered on a nearby table. Caesar's outline faded like smoke. Soon the shadows had shifted back where they'd always been.

The night visitor had vanished.

***

There's no place for a ghost on a battlefield. Too much noise for a start. Too much blood and muddle as well ... not to mention too much competition from other deaths. So it's likely that Brutus and the ghost of Caesar never did meet at Philippi. That's one story, anyway. Another is that Brutus must have seen Caesar a thousand times that day – whenever he lunged with his sword, or gave an order to his troops, or scanned the plain to direct his next attack. At any moment, with thirty-three stab wounds on show (the thirty-third being the most important), Caesar would come slinking into his head. How could a man as honest as Brutus, of all people, clear his mind of a man like Caesar?

Why would a man like Brutus want to?

Sometimes the news was good, of course. Messengers told him of a successful advance here or the capture of prisoners there. Sometimes the news was bad – of his own men in retreat or led into a trap by the enemy. 'Steady yourselves!' he would shout. 'Hold the line!'

The battle raged for hours. Only when he heard that Cassius himself had fallen did Brutus sense the tide had turned against them. 'Today was his birthday, Strato,' he told his servant.

'Cassius's birthday, sir?'

'Now his death-day, too,' said Brutus, wryly. 'Strato, will you help me leave this life in the Roman way?'

'Sir?'

'Will you grip my sword firm and true? Will you hold its point towards me and look away? Will you, Strato?'

Strato went pale. He knew what Brutus wanted. But when he saw the look in his master's eyes, he nodded. 'Give me your hand first,' he said. 'Fare you well, my lord.'

Brutus smiled. 'Farewell, good Strato – believe me, killing Caesar was twice as hard as killing myself.'

He was just in time.

At that moment, Mark Antony and Octavius rode up at the head of their troops to claim their victory. One glance at Strato and at Brutus's body told them all they needed to know. Mark Antony dismounted from his horse. He took off his helmet and sheathed his sword. Here was a young man learning fast. His words were plain and simple.

'This was the noblest Roman of them all,' he said. 'All the conspirators, apart from him, did what they did because they envied Caesar. Not Brutus. He always acted for Rome, never for himself. Let the whole world remember him and say, "This *was* an honourable man."'

The Winter's Tale

Leontes was as lucky as any man can be. He had everything in the world to make him happy. To be fair, he was well aware of this. 'I'm King of Sicilia,' he smiled. 'I have a wonderful son, Mamillius, who will become king after me. I have a perfect wife, Hermione, with another child on the way. I have Lord Camillo to help me rule my people – as good and wise a counsellor as any king could wish for ... '

Here, his smile saddened. 'And till tomorrow I have Polixenes,' he said. 'My best friend since we were boys together. I only wish he could stay here as our guest forever!'

'But he's a king, too,' said Hermione, gently. 'The King of Bohemia. He was bound to go back eventually.'

'You're tired of him, are you?'

'Not at all. But everything's packed and ready for his departure. He leaves in the morning.'

'I know,' Leontes sighed. 'And I can't persuade him otherwise – though goodness knows I've tried. Will you speak to him, Hermione? Will you keep him in Sicilia a little longer?'

Hermione looked fondly at her husband. He could be so stubborn when he had an idea fixed in his mind. 'I can't promise I'll succeed,' she said. 'But I'll certainly do my best.'

'I know you will, my dear.'

Hermione took Mamillius with her. She knew how much Polixenes liked her quiet, dreamy son. 'Maybe one day, I'll have a son of my own,' he greeted them, ruffling Mamillius's hair.

'Will he tell stories like me?' Mamillius asked. 'I love telling stories!'

'Tell us one now,' said Polixenes.

'Let me think a moment, sir. It's winter now ... and a sad tale's best for winter. Listen to this!'

The story Mamillius told really was as sad as winter ... yet somehow charming, too. His mother and his father's boyhood friend were spellbound. Maybe it was this, as much as Hermione's kind words, which made Polixenes think again. 'A few more days then,' he agreed. 'I'll stay a few more days. Everyone in Sicilia has made me so happy these last few months I can't bear to drag myself away – even to my beloved Bohemia!'

'I'll tell Leontes at once,' said Hermione.

'He'll be delighted!'

And Leontes *was* delighted.

At least, he was at first. After a while, he began to wonder. 'Why did Polixenes take no notice of me, his oldest friend?' he asked himself. 'He refused me every time when I tried to talk him round. So how did Hermione manage it? Could it be that ... ?'

He frowned, lost in thought.

He remembered Hermione laughing at the jokes Polixenes made. He remembered the fun and laughter of the parties at the palace. What he forgot was how good a hostess his Queen was – how warm and welcoming to any visitor – even now, when she was expecting their second child. Instead, a much more sinister idea took root in his mind. 'Hermione is the love of my life,' he pondered. 'I shall never tire of her. But maybe she's grown tired of me. Has my wife fallen in love with Polixenes? And is he in love with her? Is that why he agreed to stay longer?'

It was nonsense, of course.

Lord Camillo recognized this straight away. He stared at his master in dismay. 'Your Majesty,' he protested. 'Deep in my bones I know you're wrong. Not just about Queen Hermione but about King Polixenes, too. How can you believe such madness!'

'Madness?'

It was too late for Camillo to take back the word. The anger and pride of Leontes – and, yes, his stubborn streak too – already held him fast. 'Lord Camillo,' he growled. 'My wife must be put on trial and the King of Bohemia must be poisoned. That is my command. See to it.'

'But Your Majesty ... '

'Do your duty,' snarled Leontes.

'I shall, Your Majesty,' said Camillo, stiffly.

As an honest man, he had no doubt where his duty lay – and the price he would have to pay for it. With a heart as heavy as winter at its worst, he went straight to King Polixenes.

King Polixenes listened to him in horror. 'Is there nothing to be done?' he asked. 'Can't you reason with him, Camillo?'

'He's beyond reason already,' said Camillo, grimly. 'I've seen my master before in the grip of a mood like this. If I oppose him now I'll only make matters worse for the Queen and for you. For your safety's sake, Your Majesty, you must leave Sicilia at once.'

'And what of your safety, Camillo?'

'I must take a chance on that.'

'Then come to Bohemia with me. There's always room in my palace for a man as honourable as you.'

So that night they stole away – not just Polixenes, his troop of courtiers, all the baggage and all the souvenirs of a stay that had once been so splendid, but also the finest counsellor Leontes ever had. Did this bring the King of Sicilia to his senses? Not a bit of it. His fury was more monstrous than ever.

Disaster duly followed.

It began with young Mamillius. Even a storyteller as keen as he was couldn't cope with a real-life tale like this. He stopped eating. He stopped sleeping. He began to droop and pine for his mother, now in prison.

'Her only hope is a message from Delphos,' he whimpered. 'At least my father agreed to take the Oracle's advice. But suppose it doesn't arrive in time? What will happen to my mother, then?'

'She'll still have me on her side,' Paulina told him.

Mamillius looked at her gratefully. Paulina was Hermione's closest friend. If anyone could save the Queen, she could. Now Camillo was gone, Paulina's husband Antigonus was the King's chief counsellor ... a good-hearted man but not nearly as brave and quick-witted as his wife. 'Have you got a plan, Paulina?' Mamillius begged her.

'I've always got a plan,' Paulina said.

Already she'd visited the Queen in her prison cell. She'd learned that the Queen's distress had caused her to go into labour. The new baby had been born early: a lovely daughter. 'I'll present this sister of yours to the King in front of everyone,' she told Mamillius. 'If that won't melt his heart ... '

'What if it doesn't, Paulina?'

'If it doesn't?' Paulina pursed her lips. Her eyes narrowed as she considered her options. 'Then I'll make another plan,' she said.

It turned out another plan was needed. Leontes barely glanced at his newborn daughter. 'Who knows if this child is mine?' he spat. 'My false friend King Polixenes and my false wife Queen Hermione may have betrayed me from the very beginning. Antigonus, here are your orders! Take this little wretch to some lonely faraway place and leave it there to fend for itself. That's all the help it can expect from me!'

'Don't you dare do such a thing, husband!' Paulina snapped.

'Your Majesty ... ' gulped Antigonus.

'Will you obey me or not?' Leontes roared. 'Is your wife a friend of Polixenes or a friend of mine?'

'I'm a friend of yours,' said Paulina, crisply. 'But a friend you don't deserve when you behave like this.'

Antigonus was already scurrying away with the child in his arms. Paulina could hardly bear to watch him go. Worse was to come the following day, though. Leontes wanted the matter finished. 'Send for the Queen,' he commanded. 'She shall have her trial right now. And I'll be the judge and jury.'

'But what of the message from Delphos?'

'Paulina, be silent!'

The whole court was silent. The look on Leontes's face had hushed even Paulina. When the Queen, still weak from childbirth, was helped into the throne room the King showed not a flicker of sympathy. 'How do you plead, madam?' he demanded.

'Not guilty, husband,' Hermione said.

'Like Polixenes,' sneered Leontes. 'And like his henchman, Camillo. I suppose they are not guilty, too.'

'All three of us are innocent, Your Majesty.'

'All three of you are liars, you mean!'

'Not so, husband … '

Hermione's words were no more than a whisper but she spoke so firmly nobody could have missed them – or doubted that they were true. Nobody but Leontes, that is. In this mood, the truth meant nothing to him.

When, a moment later, the message finally arrived from the Oracle at Delphos, his madness was clear to all. 'Read it aloud,' he said. 'I want all Sicilia to hear of their wickedness. Then I'll pronounce my sentence.'

The messenger unrolled the parchment. He took a deep breath. Even so, there was still a catch in his voice:

'Hermione is innocent, Polixenes blameless, Camillo a true subject, Leontes a jealous tyrant ... and the King shall live without an heir if that which is lost be not found.'

King Leontes snatched at the parchment. His lips trembled as he read it for himself. He read it again and again as if he couldn't believe there was so much evil in the world. His howl echoed round the throne room.

'Is the Oracle of Delphos against me now?' he screeched. 'Has it joined forces with my enemies? At least I'll have justice here in my own kingdom. Hermione, you'll be the first to die—'

'Your Majesty! Your Majesty!'

Emilia, Hermione's lady-in-waiting, burst past the guards at the door and threw herself at Hermione's feet. Wild-eyed, she clutched at her mistress's robe. 'Mamillius is dead!' she sobbed.

'Mamillius?'

'Your troubles were too much for him, Your
Majesty. Little by little, they wore him down.
He simply … simply … '

She couldn't go on.

Nor did she need to. Queen Hermione
had collapsed. She lay face down, not moving.
Paulina was at her side in a moment. She
turned the Queen on her back, bent close and
listened. Slowly, she shook her head.

When she stood up, her eyes were on Leontes. 'Just a few breaths left,' she said. 'Soon she will be with her dead son. And who would deny her that? Emilia, help me carry this noble Queen to her resting place.'

As the door swung shut behind the two women, and the limp body they carried between them, Leontes slumped back on his throne. His lips were twitching again. He'd ripped the parchment from Delphos to shreds but it wasn't so easy to tear the Oracle's words from his mind:

'Hermione is innocent, Polixenes blameless, Camillo a true subject, Leontes a jealous tyrant ... '

But that wasn't all.

What followed was like a curse he'd laid on himself:

' ... and the King shall live without an heir if that which is lost be not found.'

The man who was once so lucky, with everything in the world to make him happy, had lost his wife, his son, his daughter. 'I killed them all,' Leontes choked. 'All three of them ... for nothing.'

***

Time is a great healer, people say. As one year faded into another – each winter into spring into summer into autumn – Sicilia grew used to their King's agony. 'Marry again,' almost everyone urged him. 'That's what Queen Hermione would have wanted.'

'I know,' agreed Leontes. 'Someone as saintly as Hermione would have forgiven even jealousy, cruelty and stupidity like mine. Tell me, though – how can I possibly forgive myself?'

Nobody had an answer for that. Not even Paulina, who watched Leontes every day as he knelt and prayed in the shrine he'd built for the wife he'd treated so badly.

From the look on Paulina's face, it was almost as if she, of all people, could find it in her heart to forgive him.

Not quite, though.

Not yet.

Fifteen years went by. In Bohemia, King Polixenes felt nothing but sadness when he thought of his boyhood friend Leontes. 'What kind of madness came over him?' he often asked Camillo, who'd become the most trusted of all his advisors. 'Why did he give way to it?'

'Madness goes its own way,' said Camillo. 'Leontes trapped himself in a rage he couldn't shake off.'

'You still miss him, Camillo? And you still miss your home country Sicilia after all these years?'

'Yes, after all these years,' Camillo nodded. 'Despite all your kindness and generosity, Your Majesty.'

'Maybe one day ... '

'One day ... '

There they broke off.

They had a more pressing problem to solve.

'Any more news of Prince Florizel?' frowned Polixenes. 'Is my son still sneaking off to see this shepherd girl – what's her name – Perdita?'

'Whenever he gets the chance,' said Camillo. 'I was wondering, Your Majesty ... '

'Yes?'

'I'm told this Perdita is no ordinary shepherd girl. She has no idea who Florizel really is. He calls himself Doricles, apparently – just a gentleman, nothing more. Yet he behaves as if it's Perdita who has royal blood. Maybe we should take a closer look. But under cover, I'd suggest. If we reveal who we really are – the King and his First Minister – we may make matters worse.'

'Disguise *ourselves* as two gentlemen, you mean?'

'Exactly,' Camillo said.

It was easier than they expected. The feast of sheep-shearing was in full swing when they arrived at Perdita's village. With so much dancing, joking and merrymaking going on,

even two cloaked and hooded strangers were warmly welcomed. 'That must be Perdita over there!' Polixenes exclaimed. 'And Florizel is with her!'

'Doricles, you mean,' Camillo reminded him.

'Doricles, yes ... '

Perdita had risen to her feet to greet them. Already, the King was charmed. 'She may not be high-born,' he whispered to Camillo. 'But she has the grace of any princess I've ever met.'

'Beautiful, too,' said Camillo.

Doricles certainly thought so. His eyes never left Perdita as she spoke to the two newcomers of animals and fruit and flowers ... as if the wealth of spring all round her could match any riches in the land. 'Ah ... I see you've fallen under my daughter's spell,' came a rough old shepherd's voice. 'Like this young man Doricles here. Or so he tells me.'

'I'd tell anyone who'll listen,' Doricles smiled.

'Tell *me*, then,' said Polixenes, still hidden

inside his hood. 'Have you promised yourself to this young woman?'

'I mean to marry her, sir.'

'Marry her?'

'If she'll have me,' Doricles said. 'And with her father's permission, of course.'

'And what of *this* father's permission?'

Savagely, Polixenes pushed back his hood. 'You're a royal prince,' he hissed. 'The son of your country's King. Accept this shepherdess if you like but you'll be rejecting me, your father!'

'Your father?' Perdita gasped.

'My father,' said Florizel, going pale. 'So you, sir, must be—'

'Lord Camillo, yes.'

The King's Minister watched in silence as Polixenes gathered his cloak around him and stalked off back to their horses. His anger seemed to be growing with every step. 'It's not the first time I've witnessed the madness of a king,' Camillo murmured. 'Perdita, Prince Florizel, wait here if you please. Good shepherd, can you spare me a moment?'

'Me, sir?'

'Yes ... you, sir.'

Camillo wasn't just honest, he was clever. Something about Perdita – her loveliness, was it? Her kindness? Her joy in simple things? – had set him wondering. He also had another gift on his side: people trusted him. Once they were alone, he said to the shepherd. 'Sir, this enchanting daughter of yours ... please tell me all about her.'

Soon Camillo had the whole story. When added to the rumours from Sicilia he'd heard over the years, this told him all he needed to know. 'So she's your *adopted* daughter,' he said, thoughtfully. 'You found her in an abandoned cradle with papers you couldn't read ... and money to pay for her upkeep. Have you still got those papers?'

'Jewels, too,' the old shepherd nodded. 'It's all there, I swear ... apart from what I spent to raise her as well as I could.'

'Better than in many a royal palace, I'm sure,' said Camillo. 'She's a credit to you, my friend. But tell me again about the man who left Perdita on these shores. He was killed, you say?'

'By a bear, my lord. Torn to pieces.'

'Poor Antigonus!'

'You knew him, sir?'

'I knew him well. Alas, he brought his death on himself but it was still a terrible way to die. Bring me the cradle, good shepherd. Along with everything that was in it.'

'Are we going somewhere, my lord?'

'On a journey, yes. A journey to my former home, Sicilia. Maybe between the four of us

– you and I, Perdita and Prince Florizel – we can do something to right a wrong which has blighted that sad country for fifteen years. Who knows, we may even right a more recent wrong!'

'By King Polixenes today, sir?'

Camillo smiled and put a finger to his lips. 'Be quick,' he said. 'We must be on our way. While you are fetching the cradle, I'll talk to Prince Florizel ... and to his sweetheart, Princess Perdita.'

'*Princess* Perdita, sir?'

'Trust me on that,' Camillo nodded.

***

There was no feast of sheep-shearing in Sicilia. In Sicilia, there'd been no feast of any kind for fifteen years. The same words haunted King Leontes constantly ... 'and the King shall live without an heir if that which is lost be not found.' Whenever he saw Paulina, his Queen's faithful servant, he lifted his hands in despair. 'You have no need to rebuke me,' he said. 'Thanks to me, you have no husband and I have no wife, no son and no daughter. Nothing you say could make me feel any worse.'

'Or any better?' said Paulina.

And she gave him a cool, appraising look as if she still had a plan or two up her sleeve.

Then, one crisp Sicilian morning at the end of spring, some visitors were shown into the palace: an old shepherd carrying a cradle, a richly-dressed nobleman with a beard as silvery as the King's, a young prince who reminded Leontes of someone ... and a girl.

Leontes stared at the girl.

He felt his heart skip a beat. No, not one beat – his heart skipped so many, he feared it may have stopped altogether. Only once before had he come across such beauty.

His lips struggled to pronounce the name. 'Hermione?' he croaked. 'Is it you? As you were when I first met you?'

Wildly, he wrenched his gaze away.

It fell on ... Polixenes? As *he* looked when the two of them first met? No, that was madness too! With a groan of despair, the King turned for help to the richly-dressed nobleman who ...

Now he gaped in utter bewilderment. 'Camillo?' he whispered. 'Are you come back to me after all these years?'

'After all these years, Your Majesty.'

Camillo's bow was as polite and tactful as ever. Quickly, he introduced the old shepherd. Three times the old man repeated his story of the princess who was marooned as a baby and showed the evidence to prove who she was.

The King shook his head in wonder. 'So that which is lost *is* found,' he murmured. 'Sicilia has an heir to the throne after all. And I have a daughter, a wonderful daughter, I believed was dead.'

'And I may have a son again,' came another kingly voice. 'That's if Florizel forgives me. Also, if Perdita's real father allows it, I'll have the best daughter-in-law a man could wish for – whether he's a king or an honest shepherd. Good day to you, Leontes, old friend.'

It was Polixenes, of course.

Just as Camillo had expected, the King of Bohemia had recovered from his fit of temper and followed the four of them to Sicilia.

Leontes was in tears as he greeted his

former comrade, embraced the daughter he'd abandoned, and met the son-in-law he knew he didn't deserve. 'If only Hermione could see this,' he wept. 'And if only I could see Hermione.'

'Maybe you can, King Leontes.'

'Paulina?'

'If you wish, come to my house at noon. I'll show you a statue I've had carved by the Italian master, Julio Romero.'

'A statue of Hermione?'

'As she would look today, Your Majesty. Older, yes. But lovelier than ever. And so lifelike, you'll be convinced she can breathe and walk and talk. Julio Romero is no ordinary sculptor.'

'And you did this for me, Paulina?'

'For you, yes ... and for the Queen who once was yours.'

'Till noon, then.'

Leontes could say no more. After all the shocks that morning, he was overwhelmed by

Paulina's gift. Only Camillo, clever Camillo, lifted the faintest of questioning eyebrows.

At noon, the atmosphere in the crowded gallery at Paulina's house felt more like a party than the viewing of a work of art. But once Paulina swished back the curtain in the corner there was pin-drop silence. There, on a plinth, stood the figure of Hermione. From the folds in her dress to the laughter lines on her face, every detail was just as it should be. Instantly, everyone was stunned. It was as if *they'd* been hand-carved, not the statue.

Leontes was first to speak. 'You're right, Paulina,' he said. 'If any statue in the world can breathe and walk and talk, it's this one. Julio Romero is a genius. If only he could bring it properly to life!'

'Really?' said Paulina, dryly. 'If he did, you'd call him a sorcerer not a sculptor. And you'd call me a witch for arranging this.'

'Never,' said Leontes.

'Never?'

'You have my word.'

'And now your word can be trusted?'

'Now and ever after, I promise,' Leontes said.

'Thank you, Your Majesty. I've been waiting for fifteen years to be sure of that. So has the blameless lady I've been sheltering in this very house. King Leontes, there's no such person as Julio Romero. He doesn't exist. Queen Hermione ... please step down from your plinth.'

'Gladly,' came the Queen's gentle voice.

She threw her arms around Perdita, allowed a kiss from Florizel, accepted the lowest of bows from Camillo and the deepest of curtsies from Paulina ... before turning at last to her husband. 'Now and ever after, I think you promised,' Hermione said.

'Now and ever after,' nodded Leontes.

There was a moment more of silence – then such a shout of approval it seemed to echo round all Sicilia.

Some say it still hovered in the air at the wedding of Perdita and Florizel and even, a little later, at the marriage of Paulina to Camillo.

It was King Leontes who brought this pair together. They were the true heroes of the winter's tale, after all. Young Mamillius himself would have recognized this if only he'd been there to tell the story.